The Sun

ELAINE LANDAU

Children's Press®
An Division of Scholastic Inc.
New York   Toronto   London   Auckland   Sydney
Mexico City   New Delhi   Hong Kong
Danbury, Connecticut

Content Consultant

Michelle Yehling

Astronomy Education Consultant

Aurora, Illinois

Reading Consultant

Cecilia Minden-Cupp, PhD

Early Literacy Consultant and Author

Library of Congress Cataloging-in-Publication Data

Landau, Elaine.
  The Sun / by Elaine Landau.
     p. cm. — (A true book)
  Includes bibliographical references and index.
  ISBN-13: 978-0-531-12568-7 (lib. bdg.)   978-0-531-14796-2 (pbk.)
  ISBN-10: 0-531-12568-8 (lib. bdg.)   0-531-14796-7 (pbk.)
  1. Sun—Juvenile literature. I. Title. II. Series.
  QB521.5.L36 2008
  523.7—dc22   2007012259

All rights reserved. Published in 2008 by Children's Press, an imprint of Scholastic Inc.
Published simultaneously in Canada. Printed in the United States of America.
SCHOLASTIC, CHILDREN'S PRESS, A TRUE BOOK, and associated logos are trademarks and/or registered trademarks of Scholastic Inc.
1 2 3 4 5 6 7 8 9 10 R 17 16 15 14 13 12 11 10 09

Find the Truth!

Everything you are about to read is true *except* for one of the sentences on this page.

Which one is **TRUE**?

T or F   The sun is the biggest object in our solar system.

T or F   Without the sun, we would still have food to eat.

Find the answer in this book.

Contents

THE BIG TRUTH!

Caught in Action!

STEREO spacecraft

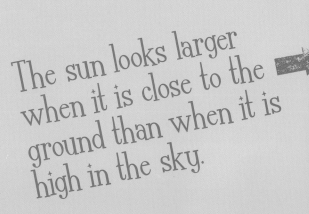

The sun looks larger when it is close to the ground than when it is high in the sky.

Bright sunlight washes out the light from other stars during the day. At night, you can see the more-distant stars shine.

CHAPTER 1

Our Special Star — The Sun

No star in our universe is actually shaped like a star.

Have you ever wished on a star? Maybe you picked a bright star in the night sky to wish on. Did you know that there is a more important star in your life? You may be surprised to learn that it is the sun.

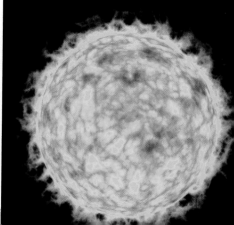

This illustration shows the hot, bright bursts of gas shooting out from the sun's surface.

Many people do not think of the sun as a star, but the sun is the closest star to Earth. It is so close that it seems brighter than any other star. It lights up the sky each day.

The sun is also the closest star to the other seven planets in Earth's **solar system**. The solar system includes the sun and everything that **orbits** it. The sun is the center of our solar system. This hot, shining star gives the planets heat and light. Without the sun, there would be no life on Earth.

The gases around the sun can get as hot as 9 million degrees Fahrenheit (5 million degrees Celsius)!

If you could drive to the sun at 55 miles per hour, your trip would take almost 200 years.

The sun is closer than other stars, but it is still very far away. It is nearly 93 million miles (150 million kilometers) from Earth. If you could survive the heat, it would take six to eight months for your spaceship to reach the sun.

Studying the Sun

3000 B.C.
The circular rock formation called Stonehenge is built, possibly to track the sun's motion through the seasons.

1543
Polish astronomer Nicolaus Copernicus's new book declares that the sun, not Earth, is the center of our solar system.

Don't plan to visit Earth's nearest star, though, even if you really like warm weather. The sun is a ball of extremely hot gas. It does not have a solid surface for a spaceship to land on. That's not even the main problem, though. No spaceship could get close to the surface. The sun is too hot. The heat would melt the ship—and everyone in it.

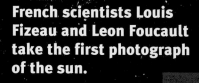

1845
French scientists Louis Fizeau and Leon Foucault take the first photograph of the sun.

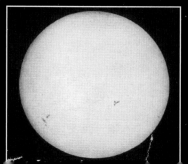

1995
The Solar and Heliospheric Observatory (SOHO) is launched. It's the first spacecraft to watch the sun all day, every day.

Venus

This photograph shows Venus passing in front of the sun, as seen from Earth. The photo was taken through a telescope with a filter that blocks the sun's dangerous rays.

CHAPTER 2

The Sun in the Solar System

If Earth were the size of the period at the end of this sentence, the sun would be the size of a golf ball.

It is hard to imagine how big the sun is. It has a **diameter** of nearly 865,000 miles (1.4 million km). More than 100 Earths could fit across the sun's face. The sun is not very big compared to other stars, though. Earth's special star is really very ordinary.

In the Middle

The sun is a medium-sized star. Some stars are much bigger, and some are much smaller. The sun is also a medium-bright star. Some stars are thousands of times brighter.

There are billions of stars in space like our sun. Many of these stars could have their own solar systems. These solar systems might include planets, space rocks called asteroids, and other space objects. These objects would orbit their star.

Earth's solar system is part of the Milky Way galaxy, shown in this photo. A galaxy is a huge group of stars and planets.

Earth looks big up close, but it is tiny compared to the sun.

More than 99 percent of the solar system's mass is in the sun.

The objects in our solar system keep circling the sun because of **gravity**. Gravity is a force that pulls objects toward each other. Every object in the universe has gravity. The more mass, or stuff, in an object, the more gravity it has. Our huge sun has enough gravity to hold all the planets in orbit.

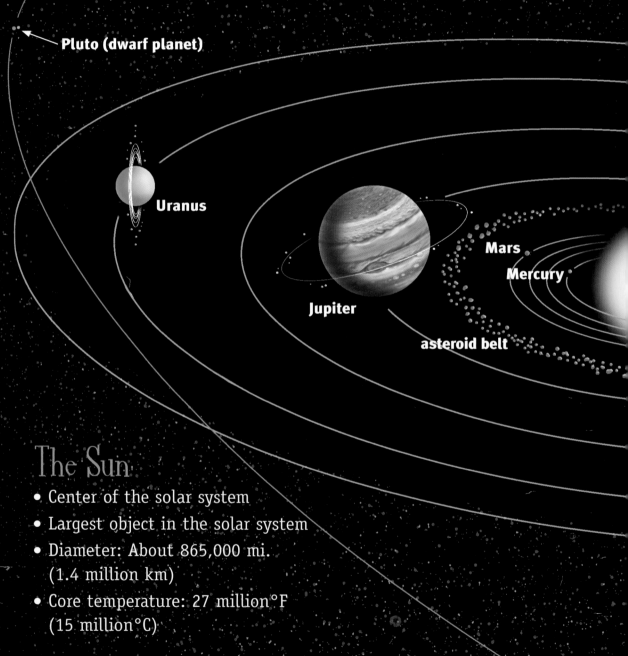

The Solar System

Pluto (dwarf planet)

Uranus

Jupiter

Mars

Mercury

asteroid belt

The Sun

- Center of the solar system
- Largest object in the solar system
- Diameter: About 865,000 mi.
  (1.4 million km)
- Core temperature: 27 million°F
  (15 million°C)

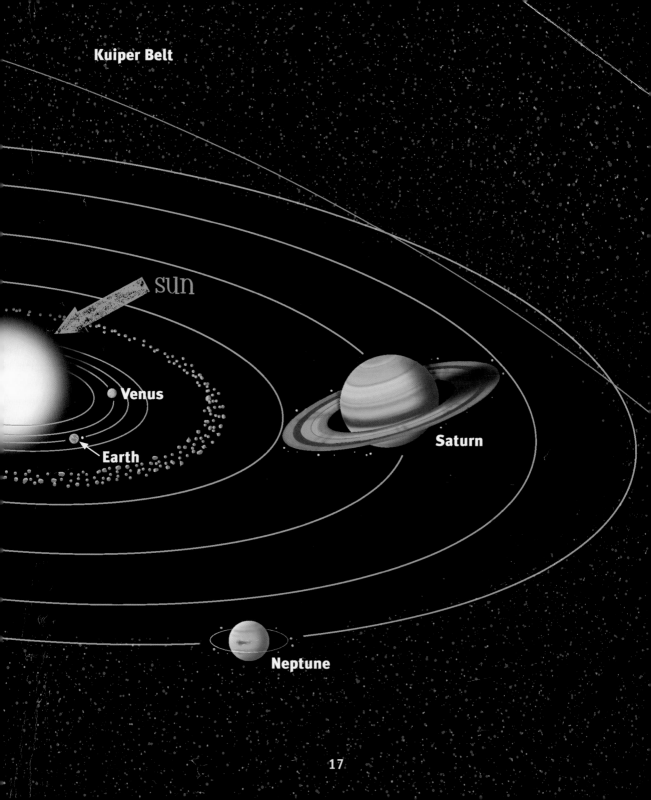

Kuiper Belt

sun

Venus

Earth

Saturn

Neptune

The Story of the Solar System

The solar system formed about five billion years ago. The sun has been at the center ever since. It all started with a huge cloud of gas, dust, and ice in space called a **nebula**. The cloud's gravity was very strong. The gravity pulled the parts of the cloud inward, toward the middle.

The collapsing cloud started to spin. The material at the center got very hot. This material formed the sun. The rest of the dust, gas, and ice started clumping together. Some of these clumps became the planets, moons, asteroids, and comets.

Here is what the solar system may have looked like as it was forming. The yellow disk is the material that would have formed the sun.

Darkness in the Daytime

What can make the sun disappear during the day? The moon can pass between Earth and the sun and block the sun's rays. This is called a **solar eclipse**. Solar eclipses can be seen from some places on Earth about once or twice a year.

These kids are using protective glasses to watch a solar eclipse.

Solar Safety

NEVER stare at the sun—even during a solar eclipse. Even a tiny bit of sunlight can badly damage your eyes.

19

In this image, the hottest areas of the sun appear almost white. The darker red areas are cooler.

CHAPTER 3

How the Sun Works

The outside of the sun is about 20 times hotter than a kitchen oven.

The sun is a very active place. The part of the sun you can see is about 10,000°F (5,500°C). Deep inside the sun, it's even hotter. At the sun's center, temperatures climb to about 27 million°F (15 million°C).

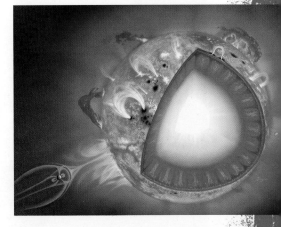

This drawing shows the sun's extremely hot center, or core.

Sending Out Energy

The sun is made mostly of gases called hydrogen and helium. Helium is the same gas that makes party balloons float in air.

What makes the sun so hot? It starts with the tiny particles that make up the sun's gases. These gas particles are very close together at the sun's core, or center. The tightly packed particles smash into each other a lot. When the particles crash, they send out energy in the form of heat and light.

Bright, glowing arcs of gas flow around sunspots.

The heat and light energy do not reach the sun's surface right away, however. It takes thousands of years for that to happen. First the energy has to

The sun's corona is visible during a total eclipse of the sun. It looks like a brilliant white ring.

travel through the huge sun. It reaches the sun's **atmosphere,** or the layer of gases that surrounds it. The energy bubbles up into the **corona,** or the outer layer of the sun's atmosphere. From there, it takes the energy only about eight minutes to reach Earth.

Many gas bubbles on the sun are as big as the state of Texas!

Sunspots

When scientists look at pictures of the sun, they often see dark patches on the bubbly surface. These patches are called sunspots. Sunspots are cooler than the rest of the sun's surface.

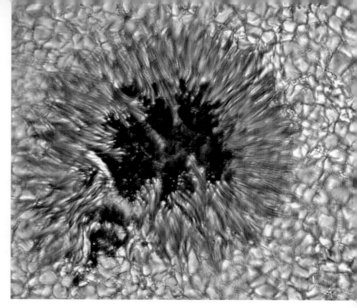

The dark area in this picture is a sunspot. The lighter regions show the bubbling gas on the sun's surface.

Many sunspots are really huge. Some are the size of Earth. Other sunspots are even bigger. A large sunspot usually lasts for a few weeks or months. Then it disappears.

Solar flares can cause power outages on Earth.

Solar Flares

Sunspots occur in areas that can also give off flashes of energy. These flashes are called solar flares. In a solar flare, huge amounts of energy and particles shoot out thousands of miles into space. Sometimes they even reach Earth's atmosphere.

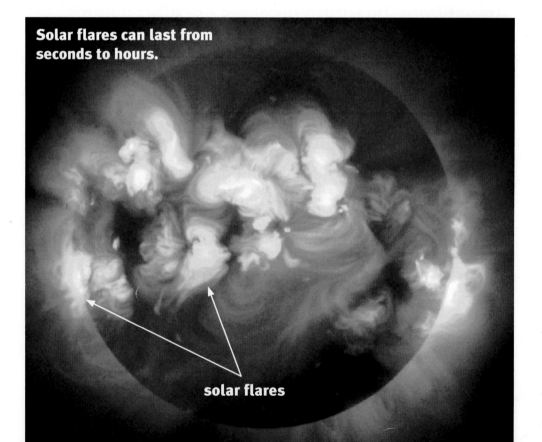

Solar flares can last from seconds to hours.

solar flares

Auroras

Solar flares can cause problems, but the sun also sends out particles more gently. These gentler streams move through space like the wind. They are called **solar wind**.

When solar wind hits the gases in Earth's atmosphere, beautiful displays of colored lights sometimes happen. These colored lights are called **auroras**. Auroras can start as a faint green glow. Then you might see bands of red, blue, and purple rippling across the sky.

Auroras occur most often in places that are far to the north or the south. Near the North and South poles on Earth, auroras can happen nearly every night.

Solar flares have caused auroras in places far from the poles, such as Texas and Florida.

An aurora known as the northern lights brightens the sky over British Columbia, Canada. *Northern lights* is the name for auroras over the northern half of Earth. These auroras are also called aurora borealis (uh-ROH-uh BOR-ee-AL-iss).

Sunspots

are cooler patches on the sun's surface.
About 15 Earths could fit inside this one!

Coronal Mass Ejections (CMEs)

are giant eruptions of gas from the sun's corona.
This one blasted more than a billion tons of gas
into space.

Caught in Action!

These photographs of the sun were taken by the Solar and Heliospheric Observatory (SOHO) spacecraft. They show four kinds of action that happen on the sun.

Solar flares

are quick explosions just above the sun's surface. They usually occur around sunspots.

Prominences

are long loops of gas that escape the sun's surface.

A hummingbird searches for food in a daisy.

CHAPTER 4

Earth and the Sun — A Perfect Pair

The sun makes life on Earth possible.

Earth happens to be in the perfect spot to benefit from the sun. The closer a planet is to the sun, the more heat it gets. Nearby planets are burning hot. Distant planets are freezing cold. Earth is not too close to and not too far from the sun. It's in just the right place for life to exist.

Plants can convert sunlight, water, and gases into food.

Water, Food, and Energy

Mars is the fourth-closest planet to the sun. It is so cold that all its water seems frozen. Earth is the third-closest planet to the sun. Earth is warm enough to keep most of its water liquid. It is easy for people to use Earth's water.

People rely on the sun for water—and much more. Without the sun, we would not have food to eat. Plants use the sun's energy to make food. Animals eat plants, or they eat other animals that eat plants. Think about the sun the next time you bite into a slice of pepperoni pizza. The sun helped bring you all the parts of the pizza!

Every day, the amount of solar energy that reaches the United States is the same amount of energy that the country uses in 1½ years.

The sun is also a big energy factory. Without it, we would not have energy to power our computers, lightbulbs, and televisions. Why? People get much of their energy from burning **fossil fuels**, such as oil and coal. Fossil fuels come from the buried remains of ancient plants. These ancient plants needed the sunlight so they could grow.

People can also use the sun's energy more directly. Special equipment can turn **solar energy** into electricity. That's a huge energy supply!

Our Weather

The sun gives us sunny days. Did you know that the sun also has a lot to do with windy and rainy days? The sun plays a role in all our weather.

The sun's energy creates wind. The energy heats up some areas of air more than others. Wind forms when this warmer air hits cooler air.

The sun's rays also make clouds by heating up Earth's oceans, rivers, and lakes. When this happens, tiny droplets of water rise. These droplets form clouds that may rain back down onto Earth.

The sun has a role in all weather, including cloud formation.

Lost Pigeons

Bad weather on the sun can cause serious problems. It can can even confuse homing pigeons.

Some people race homing pigeons. Homing pigeons are good at finding their way home. Pigeon racers take their birds to far-off places. Then they see how long it takes the pigeons to return home. The fastest pigeon wins.

How does a pigeon find its way? Scientists think pigeons are like flying **compasses**. Bad solar weather can confuse the birds' "internal compass." When this happens, pigeons don't know which way is north. As a result, a lot of the birds get lost.

Scientists are looking for ways to predict solar weather. If they succeed, it will solve a lot of problems—including helping pigeon racers know when to release their birds.

The *Genesis* spacecraft flew toward the sun to capture particles that the sun gives off.

CHAPTER 5

How Astronomers Study the Sun

Genesis sent back the first space materials since astronauts went to the moon more than 35 years ago.

Astronomers, scientists who study space, are eager to learn more about the sun. They know that the sun is too hot to get close to. Instead, astronomers found clever ways to study the sun from afar. How did they do it? Two exciting missions were called *Genesis* and *STEREO*.

Genesis

Astronomers at the National Aeronautics and Space Administration (NASA) decided to capture the wind. In 2001, they sent a spacecraft called *Genesis* to bring back samples of solar wind. Solar wind is made of tiny particles. The spacecraft captured solar wind particles on metallic glass plates. It collected a sample the size of a few grains of sand before sending it to Earth in 2004.

Astronomers will continue to study solar wind. It will help them learn what made up the nebula that first formed the solar system. Solar wind may still contain particles left over from this original cloud.

Solar wind travels at about 1 million miles per hour.

Genesis sent a container with solar wind particles to Earth in 2004. The container had a hard landing in the Utah desert, but the samples arrived safely back on Earth.

Each of the two *STEREO* spacecraft holds cameras and other instruments to observe the sun. These spacecraft could help scientists learn to predict solar weather.

STEREO

NASA launched a new set of spacecraft toward the sun in October 2006. The two-year mission to observe the sun is called *STEREO*. One of the spacecraft, *STEREO A*, orbits the sun ahead of Earth. The other, *STEREO B*, orbits the sun behind Earth. Together, the spacecraft have delivered the first-ever 3-D images of the sun.

Astronomers hope to use these images to track solar weather as it travels from the sun to Earth. Then people will know when a big solar storm is heading toward Earth.

STEREO will study bursts of energy from the sun that put astronauts in danger.

This image was created by combining images taken by both *STEREO* spacecraft.

Our giant sun is still full of mysteries for astronomers to solve. We already know a lot about how it affects everyday life on our planet. We know that every day, in many ways, the sun helps us survive. ★

The sun sets over the Sahara Desert in Africa.

True Statistics

Age: About five billion years

Diameter: About 865,000 mi. (1.4 million km)

Mass: Equal to the mass of about 333,000 Earths

Distance from Earth: About 93 million mi. (150 million km)

100-watt lightbulbs needed to make as much light: 3,827,000,000,000,000,000,000,000

Time it takes to orbit the galaxy: 230 million Earth years

Surface temperature: 10,000°F (5,500°C)

Core temperature: 27 million°F (15 million°C)

Time it takes for sunlight to reach Earth: 8.5 minutes

Did you find the truth?

T The sun is the biggest object in our solar system.

F Without the sun, we would still have food to eat.

Resources

Books

Birch, Robin. *Sun*. New York: Chelsea House Publications, 2003.

Chrismer, Melanie. *The Sun*. Danbury, CT: Children's Press, 2008.

Craig, Gary. *Where Does the Sun Go?* Chehalis, WA: Elora Media, 2006.

Hill, Steele, and Michael Carlowicz. *The Sun*. New York: Harry N. Abrams, Inc., 2006.

Petersen, Christine. *Solar Power*. Danbury, CT: Children's Press, 2004.

Prinja, Raman K. *The Sun*. Chicago: Heinemann Library, 2003.

Royston, Angela. *The Day the Sun Went Out: The Sun's Energy*. Austin, TX: Raintree Steck-Vaughn, 2005.

Shearer, Deborah A. *Space Missions*. Mankato, MN: Bridgestone Books, 2002.

Walpole, Brenda. *I Wonder Why the Sun Rises and Other Questions about Time and Seasons*. New York: Kingfisher Books, 2006.

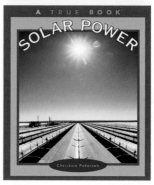

Organizations and Web Sites

American Museum of Natural History—OLogy
Astronomy: Our Place in Space
ology.amnh.org/astronomy/index.htm
Try fun activities and explorations.

Solar and Heliospheric Observatory (SOHO) Free Stuff Page
soho.nascom.nasa.gov/freestuff/
Get a screen saver, real-time image viewer, and more.

Space Weather Center
www.spaceweathercenter.org
Go here for information on solar weather. Don't miss the fun space games.

Places to Visit

Kennedy Space Center
Kennedy Space Center, FL 32899
www.ksc.nasa.gov
Explore NASA's launch headquarters and learn more about some of the organization's space missions.

Smithsonian National Air and Space Museum
Independence Avenue at 4th Street, SW
Washington, DC 20560
202-633-1000
www.nasm.si.edu
Here you'll find space suits, spacecraft, moon rocks, and other exciting things.

Important Words

atmosphere (AT-mu-sfihr) – the blanket of gases that surrounds a planet or other object

auroras (uh-ROR-uhz) – displays of colored lights in the sky

compasses (KUHM-puhss-ehz) – instruments for finding directions, with a magnetic needle that always points north

corona (kuh-ROH-nuh) – the outermost layer of the sun's atmosphere

diameter (dye-A-muh-tur) – the distance across the center of a round object

fossil fuels – fuels formed from the remains of ancient living things

gravity – a force that pulls two objects together

nebula (NE-byuh-luh) – a huge cloud of gas and dust in space where stars may form

orbits – travels around an object such as a sun or planet

solar eclipse – when the moon blocks the view of the sun from parts of Earth

solar energy – energy that comes from the sun and can be made into other forms of useful energy

solar system – a sun and all the objects that travel around it

solar wind – particles flowing outward from the sun

Index

About the Author

Award-winning author Elaine Landau has a bachelor's degree from New York University and a master's degree in library and information science from Pratt Institute.

She has written more than 300 non-fiction books for children and young adults. Although Ms. Landau often writes on science topics, she especially likes writing about planets and space.

She lives in Miami, Florida, with her husband and son. The trio can often be spotted at the Miami Museum of Science and Space Transit Planetarium. You can visit Elaine Landau at her Web site: www.elainelandau.com.

PHOTOGRAPHS © 2008: AP Images/Steve Holland: 33; Corbis Images: 12 (Mian Khursheed/Reuters), 30 (Joe McDonald), 19 bottom (Doug Menuez), 10 left (Skyscan); Getty Images: 10 right (Imagno/Hulton Archive), 35 (Stockbyte), cover, back cover (StockTrek/Photodisc); Index Stock Imagery, Inc/ThinkStock: 8; Masterfile/Bill Frymire: 13; NASA: 11 right (European Space Agency), 25, 29 top (JAXA), 36, 39 (JPL), 11 left (National Science Foundation), 24 top (NSO/NOAO), 20, 28 bottom, 28 top, 29 bottom (SOHO), 4 bottom, 14, 19 top, 22, 23, 40, 41; Pat Rasch: 16, 17; Photo Researchers, NY: 4 top, 15 (Roger Harris), 7 (Gregory MacNicol), 5 bottom, 42 (Daniele Pellegrini), 21 (Publiphoto), 3, 9, 18 (Detlev van Ravenswaay); Scholastic Library Publishing, Inc.: 44; Superstock, Inc.: 5 top, 27, 31 (age fotostock), 6 (Mauritius), 34 (Prisma).